ACCENT ON ACHIEVEMENT

Mark
Williams

The "Keys" to Success: Progressive Technical & Rhythmic Studies in all 12 Major and 12 Minor Keys

Dear Band Student:

Congratulations on completing the first two books of
ACCENT ON ACHIEVEMENT. Book 3 will help you to develop
the musical and technical skills necessary for a lifetime of great
music-making. Your "Keys" to success include scales,
exercises and fun tunes in all 12 major and 12 minor keys.
You'll learn new rhythms and meters, and also improve your
tone and intonation while playing a rich variety of chorales.
With diligent practice, there's no end to what you can accomplish!
We wish you the best in your quest for musical excellence.

John O'Reilly   Mark Williams

Instrument photos (cover and page 1) are courtesy of Yamaha Corporation of America.

ACCENT ON CONCERT B♭ MAJOR

CHORALE: CHILDREN'S PRAYER from "HANSEL AND GRETEL"

Engelbert Humperdinck
(1854–1921)

B♭ MAJOR SCALE (CONCERT B♭)

INTERVAL WORKOUT

SCALE STUDY

CHROMATIC SCALE

ACCENT ON RHYTHM: 9/8 Time

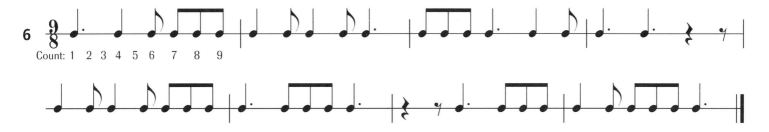

Count: 1 2 3 4 5 6 7 8 9

MORNING HAS BROKEN

Irish Folk Song

Moderato

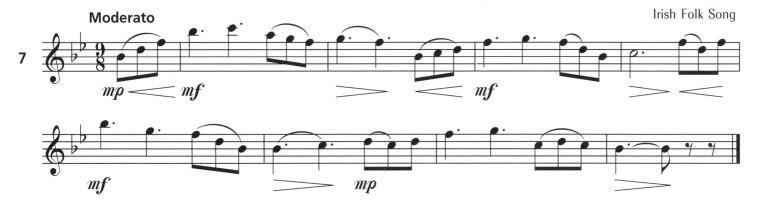

ACCENT ON RHYTHM: 12/8 Time

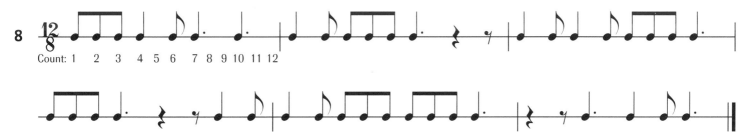

Count: 1 2 3 4 5 6 7 8 9 10 11 12

ANDANTE CANTABILE from "SYMPHONY NO. 5"

Peter I. Tchaikovsky
(1840–1893)

ACCENT ON CONCERT G MINOR

CHORALE: BASED ON A THEME BY NEUMARK

Johann Sebastian Bach
(1685–1750)

G MELODIC MINOR SCALE (CONCERT G)

INTERVAL WORKOUT

SCALE STUDY

G HARMONIC MINOR SCALE (CONCERT G)

ACCENT ON RHYTHM: 3/2 Time

15

Count: 1 & 2 & 3 (e) & a

RONDO

Henry Purcell
(1659–1695)

16 Maestoso

f

mf

Fine

p

mf

D. C. al Fine

THE WILD HORSEMAN

Robert Schumann
(1810–1856)

17 Allegro

mf

Fine

mp

D. C. al Fine

ACCENT ON CONCERT E♭ MAJOR

CHORALE: BE THOU MY VISION

Traditional Irish Melody

E♭ MAJOR SCALE (CONCERT E♭)

INTERVAL WORKOUT

SCALE STUDY

ACCENT ON CONCERT E♭ MAJOR

CHROMATIC SCALE

ACCENT ON RHYTHM: ♫.

23

Count: 1 & 2 & 1 e(&a)2 &

THE KEEL ROW

Allegretto

English/Scottish Folk Song

24

mf

f

ACCENT ON RHYTHM: ♫♩ and ♩♫♫

25

Count: 1 e (&)a 2 & 1 & a (2) e &

PETITE OISEAU

Moderato

Traditional

26

mp

mf

ACCENT ON CONCERT C MINOR

CHORALE: PRELUDE IN C MINOR

Frèdèric Chopin
(1810–1849)

C MELODIC MINOR SCALE (CONCERT C)

INTERVAL WORKOUT

SCALE STUDY

C HARMONIC MINOR SCALE (CONCERT C)

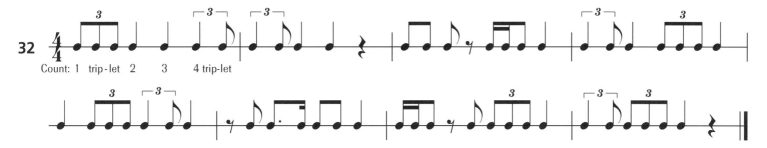

Three Ways to Swing It

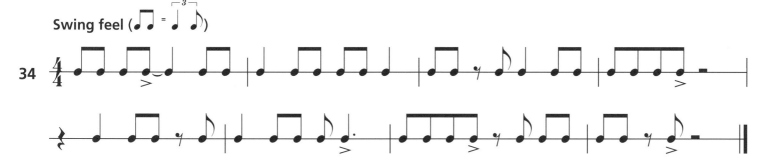

The Battle of Jericho

American Spiritual

ACCENT ON CONCERT F MAJOR

CHORALE: SINE NOMINE

Ralph Vaughan Williams
(1872–1958)

Maestoso

36
mf

f

rit.   mf

F MAJOR SCALE (CONCERT F)

37

INTERVAL WORKOUT

*

38

*See Fingering Chart on page 38.

SCALE STUDY

39

CHROMATIC SCALE

40

ACCENT ON RHYTHM: ♫ in 6/8 Time

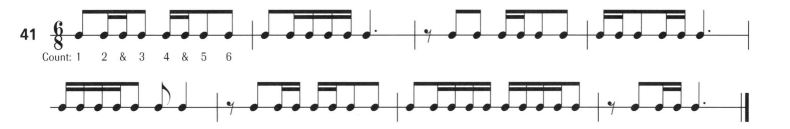

Count: 1 2 & 3 4 & 5 6

THE IRISH WASHERWOMAN

Allegro

Traditional

LIP SLUR/FLEXIBILITY STUDY

ACCENT ON CONCERT D MINOR

CHORALE: PICARDY

17th Century French Melody

Accent on Rhythm: ♪. ♪♪♪ in 6/8 Time

49 Count: 1 2 & 3 4 5 6

Greensleeves

English Folk Song

50 Andante

mp

mf

mp   *mf*   *mp*

Accent on Rhythm: ♪ (Sixteenth Rest)

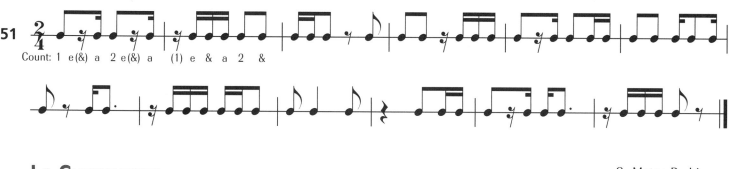

51 Count: 1 e (&) a 2 e (&) a (1) e & a 2 &

La Cumparsita

G. Matos Rodriguez
(1897–1948)

52 Moderato

mf

f

ACCENT ON CONCERT A♭ MAJOR

CHORALE: HOW FIRM A FOUNDATION

Early American Melody

53 Moderato

mf

mp

mf

rit.

A♭ MAJOR SCALE (CONCERT A♭)

54

*See Fingering Chart on page 38.

INTERVAL WORKOUT

55

SCALE STUDY

56

CHROMATIC SCALE

57

*See Fingering Chart on page 38.

ACCENT ON RHYTHM: $\frac{5}{4}$ and $\frac{6}{4}$ Time

PROMENADE from "PICTURES AT AN EXHIBITION"

Modest Mussorgsky
(1839–1881)

WALTZ from "SYMPHONY NO. 6"

Peter I. Tchaikovsky
(1840–1893)

ACCENT ON CONCERT F MINOR

CHORALE: THE GOD OF ABRAHAM PRAISE

Hebrew Folk Song

61 Moderato
mf
mp
mf
rit.

F MELODIC MINOR SCALE (CONCERT F)

62

INTERVAL WORKOUT

63

SCALE STUDY

64

F HARMONIC MINOR SCALE (CONCERT F)

65

ACCENT ON RHYTHM:

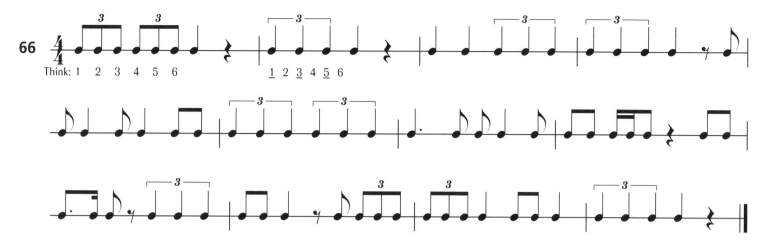

66

Think: 1 2 3 4 5 6

SOMETIMES I FEEL LIKE A MOTHERLESS CHILD

Largo

American Spiritual

67

TRIPLET TUNE

Maestoso

68

ACCENT ON CONCERT C MAJOR

CHORALE: IT IS WELL

Phillip Bliss
(1838–1876)

Moderato

C MAJOR SCALE (CONCERT C)

*See Fingering Chart on page 38.

INTERVAL WORKOUT

SCALE STUDY

CHROMATIC SCALE

*See Fingering Chart on page 38.

ACCENT ON RHYTHM: *Changing Meters —* $\frac{2}{4}$ *through* $\frac{6}{4}$

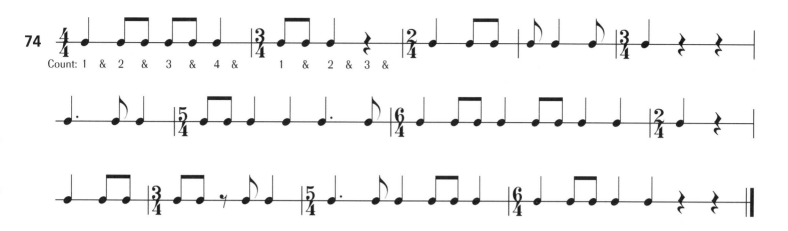

Count: 1 & 2 & 3 & 4 &   1 & 2 & 3 &

SOLILOQUY

LIP SLUR/FLEXIBILITY STUDY

ACCENT ON CONCERT A MINOR

CHORALE: BASED ON A THEME BY HASSLER

Johann Sebastian Bach
(1685–1750)

A MELODIC MINOR SCALE (CONCERT A)

INTERVAL WORKOUT

SCALE STUDY

A HARMONIC MINOR SCALE (CONCERT A)

ACCENT ON CONCERT Db MAJOR

CHORALE: LONDONDERRY AIR

Irish Folk Song

ACCENT ON RHYTHM: *Changing Meters* — 6/8 *and* 2/4

WASSAIL SONG

Traditional Carol

ACCENT ON RHYTHM: *Changing Meters* — 6/8 *and* 3/4

FIESTA MARIACHI

ACCENT ON CONCERT B♭ MINOR

CHORALE: KOMM, SÜSSER TOD

Johann Sebastian Bach
(1685–1750)

B♭ MELODIC MINOR SCALE (CONCERT B♭)

INTERVAL WORKOUT

SCALE STUDY

B♭ HARMONIC MINOR SCALE (CONCERT B♭)

ACCENT ON RHYTHM: 5/8 Time

99

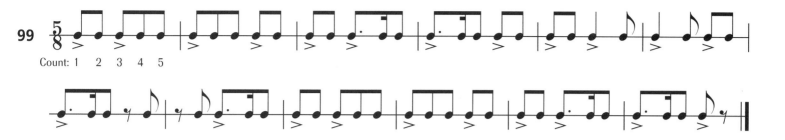

Count: 1 2 3 4 5

FUN WITH FIVE

Moderato

100

ACCENT ON RHYTHM: Changing Meters with 3/8, 5/8

101

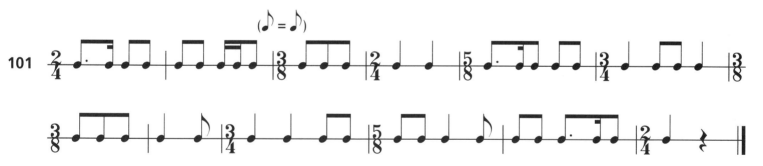

VARIATIONS ON A STAR SONG

Moderato

102

Count: 1 2 3 4 5 6 7

ACCENT ON CONCERT G MAJOR

ACCENT ON CONCERT E MINOR

E MELODIC MINOR SCALE (CONCERT E)

INTERVAL WORKOUT

E HARMONIC MINOR SCALE (CONCERT E)

LA CINQUANTAINE

J. Gabriel-Marie
(1852–1928)

Allegretto

ACCENT ON CONCERT G♭ MAJOR

G♭ MAJOR SCALE (CONCERT G♭)

INTERVAL WORKOUT

CHROMATIC SCALE

MICHAEL, ROW THE BOAT ASHORE

American Spiritual

Andante

MARCH OF THE MEN OF HARLECH

Welsh Folk Song

Moderato

ACCENT ON CONCERT E♭ MINOR

ACCENT ON CONCERT D MAJOR

D MAJOR SCALE (CONCERT D)

121

INTERVAL WORKOUT

122

CHROMATIC SCALE

123

ALLELUIA

17th Century Melody

Moderato

124

SHENANDOAH

American Folk Song

Adagio

125

ACCENT ON CONCERT B MINOR

B MELODIC MINOR SCALE (CONCERT B)

126

INTERVAL WORKOUT

127

B HARMONIC MINOR SCALE (CONCERT B)

128

HATIKVAH

Israeli National Anthem

129

ACCENT ON CONCERT A MAJOR

A MAJOR SCALE (CONCERT A)

130

*See Fingering Chart on page 38.

INTERVAL WORKOUT

131

CHROMATIC SCALE

132

BINGO

American Folk Song

Allegro

133

f

MY BONNIE LIES OVER THE OCEAN

Moderato

Traditional

134

mf

ACCENT ON CONCERT F♯/G♭ MINOR

F♯ MELODIC MINOR SCALE (CONCERT F♯)

135

INTERVAL WORKOUT

136

F♯ HARMONIC MINOR SCALE (CONCERT F♯)

137

THEME from "SCHEHERAZADE"

Nicolai Rimsky-Korsakov
(1844–1908)

138

ACCENT ON CONCERT C♭ MAJOR

C♭ MAJOR SCALE (CONCERT C♭)

139

INTERVAL WORKOUT

140

CHROMATIC SCALE

141

THE BLUEBELLS OF SCOTLAND

Scottish Folk Song

Moderato

142

mf

f

mf

BEAUTIFUL DREAMER

Stephen Foster
(1826–1864)

Andantino

143

mp

1.

2.

mf   *mp*

rit.

p

ACCENT ON CONCERT A♭ MINOR

A♭ MELODIC MINOR SCALE (CONCERT A♭)

INTERVAL WORKOUT

A♭ HARMONIC MINOR SCALE (CONCERT A♭)

HAVA NAGILA

Hebrew Folk Song

ACCENT ON CONCERT E MAJOR

E MAJOR SCALE (CONCERT E)

148

INTERVAL WORKOUT

149

CHROMATIC SCALE

150

HOME ON THE RANGE

American Folk Song

151

ACCENT ON CONCERT C#/Db MINOR

C# MELODIC MINOR SCALE (CONCERT C#)

152

INTERVAL WORKOUT

153

C# HARMONIC MINOR SCALE (CONCERT C#)

154

WE THREE KINGS

Moderato

Traditional Carol

155

FLUTE FINGERING CHART

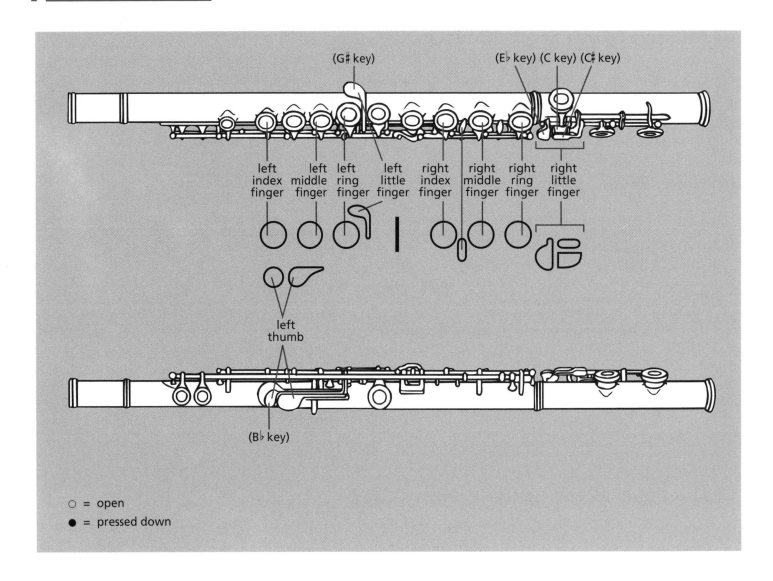

○ = open
● = pressed down

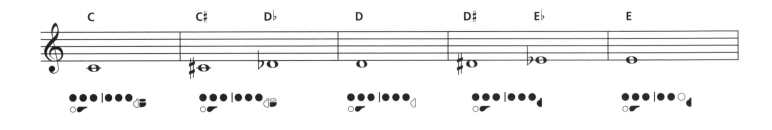

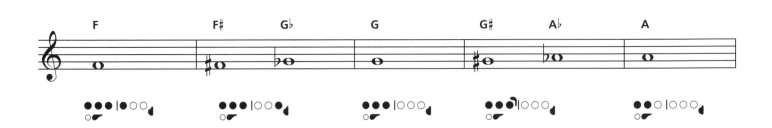

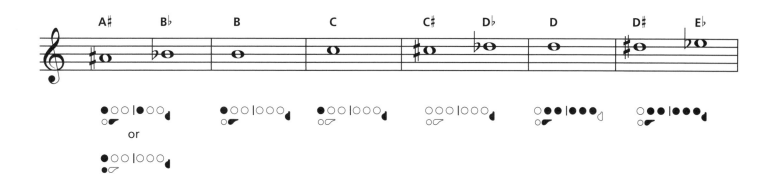

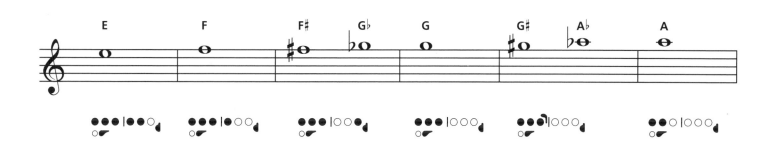

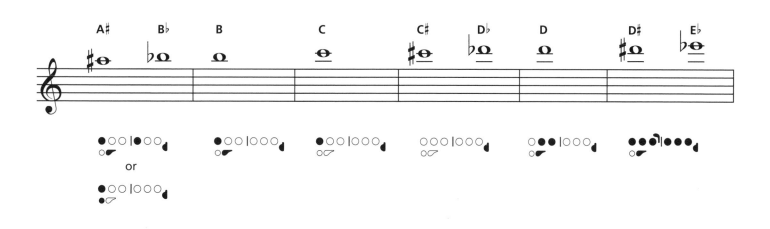

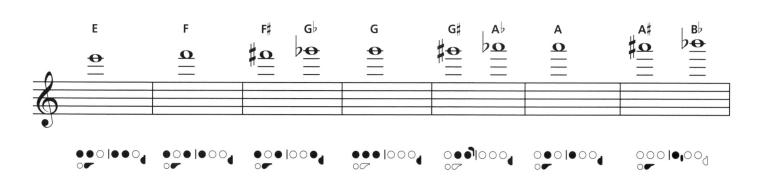

HOME PRACTICE RECORD

Week	Date	ASSIGNMENT	Mon	Tue	Wed	Thur	Fri	Sat	Sun	Total	Parent Signature
1											
2											
3											
4											
5											
6											
7											
8											
9											
10											
11											
12											
13											
14											
15											
16											
17											
18											
19											
20											
21											
22											
23											
24											
25											
26											
27											
28											
29											
30											
31											
32											
33											
34											
35											
36											